Walking with the Son of Man

A Study of Luke

Wes and Elaine Willis

ACCENT PUBLICATIONS
Colorado Springs, Colorado

Accent Publications
P.O. Box 36640
7125 Disc Drive
Colorado Springs, Colorado   80936

Library of Congress Catalog Card Number 95-75830

ISBN 0-89636-315-5

CONTENTS

Introduction to the Gospel of Luke

Who was Luke? Luke was not one of the twelve apostles. Rather, he was a Gentile, which gave him a different perspective from the other gospel writers. Luke also was a physician, which is seen in certain recurring themes that emerge throughout his writings. But Luke is perhaps best known as an historian who meticulously gathered and compiled information for our eternal benefit.

Why did Luke write his Gospel? Obviously, the Holy Spirit led Luke to write what God wanted. But under the Spirit's direction, Luke included many features that contribute to the uniqueness of this book. More than any of the other Gospel writers, Luke emphasized the humanity of Christ (without minimizing His deity), tracing His genealogy all the way from Adam. This also is seen in his focus on Jesus as the Son of Man. Luke included many details about Christ's ministry to the Gentiles after the Jews rejected Him. He emphasized the importance of women and children, and he included many personal, human interest elements, as one might expect of a physician.

This Gospel, the first of Luke's two books, records Christ's earthly ministry. Acts, the second of his two books, presents the continuation of that ministry after Christ ascended into Heaven. Together, these books describe the events surrounding Christ's sacrifice and the establishment and growth of the church.

Luke states his purpose for writing in Luke 1:1-4. He wanted to write an orderly account of the life and ministry of Jesus so that the reader (verse 4) might believe with confidence. May this happen as you study this magnificent Gospel—the Gospel of Jesus Christ, the Son of Man.

1

"THAT'S RIGHT, SON. THE WISE MEN JUST BROUGHT GOLD, FRANKINCENSE, AND MYRRH. NO TOYS."

The Son of Man Comes to Earth
LUKE 1—2

Anticipation and rejoicing usually accompany the birth of a child. When each of our three sons was born, we experienced both.

With each one we first experienced anticipation as we waited to find out if conception had occurred. Once that was confirmed, the *real* waiting began—many more months of it! Finally the wait was over. A new child entered the world. In our family, each baby was a healthy boy, and we rejoiced. We announced the event with the enthusiasm of freshman parents—phone calls, announcements, and personal visits. "Spread the news! Tell the world! We have a(nother) son!"

Not all of the elements of our experience are paralleled in the births of John and Jesus. There was no wondering if conception would occur. In each family at least one parent was told that conception would occur. And one was conceived without any sexual contact!

But the nine long months of waiting were the same. Each mother waited, wondered, hoped, and planned. Finally, that special day came—first for Elizabeth, and three months later, for Mary. Elizabeth, surrounded by friends and neighbors, shared her joy with loved ones.

But for Mary, the birth was different. Away from home on a trip, in a setting shared with animals, helped and comforted only by a brand-new husband, she bore her Son, the Messiah. But God rejoiced! And He sent His messengers—angels to herald the good news! Mary's family was not there to share her joy, so God sent representatives of the family of man. Shepherds—crude and common, but good people—shared God's and Mary's joy. Their adoration was a foreshadowing of things to come, for many common people would flock to Jesus to love, serve, and follow Him. They would be His emissaries to tell the world that the Messiah had come. Salvation is here; God is in our midst!

REASON FOR WRITING
(Luke 1:1-4)

*L*uke begins his Gospel by explaining how he got his information and why he wrote the book.

1. (1:2-3) *In addition to perhaps having copies of Matthew and Mark, what sources did Luke draw on to gather information about the birth and ministry of Jesus?*

2. (1:3-4) *What are the reasons Luke gives for wanting to write his account?*

❐ *What advantages does a written account have over oral tradition as the years pass?*

❐ *What difference does it make to us today that we have the written Word of God, rather than stories shared verbally from generation to generation:*

— as individuals?

— as families?

— as churches?

ANNOUNCEMENT OF JOHN THE BAPTIST (Luke 1:5-25)

*T*his section describes the angel's announcement to Zecharias that John would be conceived. Zecharias, because of his doubt-induced questioning, remained mute until he named the baby John.

1. (1:5-7) *Who were Zecharias and Elizabeth?*

2. (1:8-18) *What were some of the reasons that Zecharias found it so hard to believe?*

3. (1:19-20) *What do you think might have been accomplished by the penalty for Zecharias's unbelief?*

4. (1:21-25) *Why is Zecharias and Elizabeth's reaction after they learned of her pregnancy significant?*

ANNOUNCEMENT OF JESUS, GOD'S SON (Luke 1:26-56)

After Gabriel's announcement to Mary that she would conceive, Mary visited her cousin Elizabeth to share her joy. This section includes Mary's song of praise.

1. (1:29,34,38) *Mary and Joseph's engagement was a legally binding marriage contract, but it excluded sexual contact until after the marriage ceremony. As indicated by her responses, what emotions do you think Mary felt as she talked with the angel?*

❐ List Mary's statements or questions in response to Gabriel. In what other ways might she have responded?

What Mary said   **_Other possible responses_**

❐ How does Mary's response to God's messenger contrast with Zecharias's response?

3. (1:39-45; cf. John 1:29) What are some of the implications of the fact that John (in Elizabeth's womb) responded to Jesus (in Mary's womb) when Mary approached?

4. (1:42-45) What did Elizabeth understand about Jesus based on the blessing she gave to Mary?

5. (1:46-56) This hymn of praise (often called the Magnificat) is a remarkable example of theology and poetry. What were some of the main reasons why Mary praised God?

BIRTH OF JOHN THE BAPTIST
(Luke 1:57-80)

*L*uke begins this passage by recounting John's birth and naming. After God removed Zecharias's penalty, he praised God and prophesied of John's future.

1. (1:57-61) *Circumcision, traditionally done eight days after birth, was the sign of the Abrahamic covenant and symbolized spiritual commitment to God. How did the friends and neighbors of Zecharias and Elizabeth feel about the birth and naming of John?*

2. (1:62-66) *Why do you think the relatives and neighbors marvelled?*

3. (1:67-79) *What are the main emphases of Zecharias's prophecy?*

4. (1:76-79) *Look at Zecharias's expectations for his son. How were these fulfilled in the life of John the Baptist?*

BIRTH AND PRESENTATION OF JESUS
(Luke 2:1-39)

*T*his passage includes Luke's account of the birth of Jesus and His subsequent presentation in the temple, where both Simeon and Anna predicted Jesus' future ministry.

1. (2:1-7) *Compare Micah 5:2. Why is it significant that Jesus was born in Bethlehem among animals, without fanfare?*

2. (2:8-20) *In Bible times, shepherds usually were rugged and coarse persons, with little social status or power. Why might God have chosen shepherds to be the first to hear and share Jesus' birth?*

❒ *How could it encourage us to recognize that Jesus was born to ordinary common people, without rank or status, and His birth was announced through shepherds?*

3. (2:25-38) *What are the main points of Simeon's and Anna's prophecies?*

THE BOYHOOD OF JESUS
(Luke 2:40-52)

*T*he final part of this passage gives some insight into the boyhood of Jesus, including His discussion with religious leaders at age 12.

1. **(2:41-46)** *Jesus undoubtedly went up to Jerusalem for Passover with His parents and extended family. Since aunts, uncles, cousins, and others were together, they probably were looking after each other's children. What are some of the emotions Jesus' parents probably felt when they finally missed Him?*

❒ *Why do you think Jesus, the perfect Son of God who could not act improperly, stayed behind without telling His parents when He knew it would cause them concern?*

2. **(2:47-48)** *The teachers and Jesus' parents were astonished at Jesus' knowledge. Why do you think the teachers did not recognize who He was then? What do you think they felt about a 12-year-old boy who had such insight?*

❒ *Why do you think this is the only recorded incident of Jesus' childhood God included in Scripture?*

3. **(2:49-52)** *Even though Jesus was the Son of God, He recognized His duty to obey His earthly parents. What does Jesus' answer in verse 49 indicate about His self-understanding of His mission?*

❏ *What does it reveal about His deity and His humanity?*

DIGGING DEEPER

1. *The way in which we respond to God and to His Word is a very important theme throughout the gospel of Luke. The first two chapters of Luke present several examples of different responses to God's Word. Zecharias found it hard to believe God's message. In what areas of your life have you found it hard to trust God?*

2. *Notice Mary's response to God's messenger (1:26-38). What activities or experiences have helped build your faith to the place where you can respond more like Mary?*

3. *Jesus grew (2:49,52) in spirit and wisdom, in God's grace, and in favor with God and man. His example of obedience, even as a 12-year-old, establishes a perfect model for us to follow. What can you do to develop similar attitudes toward God?*

4. *Think of Zecharias's attitude toward his son at birth. Name some specific ways that parents or teachers today could encourage young children to look forward to service for God.*

2

"IF YOU'RE GOING TO STAY ON THAT DIET OF YOURS, YOU CAN'T HAVE ALL THIS TEMPTATION AROUND."

Jesus Begins His Ministry
LUKE 3—4

*S*ome years ago I visited in the home of a great theologian—a man widely respected for analytical thinking, insightful teaching, and brilliant repartee. But on that day, as we relaxed in his home, I observed a different man. This usually reasonable, logical, organized, calm man was reduced to a frustrated mass of anxiety by the behavior of his irrational, illogical, emotional, young children. Finally he called out to his wife, "Will you please take care of your children!"

Yet this man remained a theologian's theologian. His logic was flawless, his expression precise, and his debate relentless. His graduate students never knew about that incident; and if they had, it would not have mattered. His skills were not diminished in the least; in the classroom he was king.

At home—that's another story. To his kids, he was just plain old "Daddy." His children couldn't have cared less about his insight, skill, or reputation. Those who knew him best demonstrated that a prophet *is* without honor in his own country.

Jesus Christ taught and clearly demonstrated this principle at the start of His ministry. "Verily I say unto you, No prophet is accepted in his own country" (Luke 4:24). Although He came as God's only begotten Son, many of those who knew Him best rejected Him. Yet He chose to minister to those very people and to love them, even to the ultimate expression of that love—dying for them.

JOHN'S CALL FOR REPENTANCE
(Luke 3:1-22)

*J*ohn's ministry was to prepare the way for the Messiah—calling the nation to repentance. It included the privilege of baptizing Jesus.

1. (3:1-9,16) *John the Baptist lived in the desert, fulfilling the prophecy in Isaiah 40:3-5. What message did John proclaim?*

2. (3:10-14) *According to John, what kinds of actions or lifestyle indicated true repentance and righteousness? What could be parallel actions today?*

1st Century actions   **Similar actions today**

17

3. (3:8-9,17) *What kinds of judgment did John predict for those who remained complacent in their sin?*

4. (3:18-20) *Herod was living with Herodias, the wife of his half-brother Philip. Why was John put into prison?*

5. (3:21-22) *Why do you think Jesus went to John to be baptized?*

❐ *Only Luke mentions that Jesus was praying at His baptism. What might be the significance of this?*

THE GENEALOGY OF JESUS
(Luke 3:23-38)

*T*his record of Jesus' earthly ancestors traces His lineage all the way back to Adam. It is probably Mary's genealogy, showing Jesus' right to be Messiah through the physical line.

1. (3:23) *Why would God the Holy Spirit have had Luke include the phrase, "being (as was supposed) the son of Joseph"?*

2. (3:34-38) *Why might Luke extend Jesus' genealogy beyond Abraham to Adam? (Matthew, who emphasized Jesus' Jewish heritage in his gospel, only records back to Abraham.)*

❏ *How does this fit with his emphasis on Jesus as Son of Man?*

❏ *What is the significance to you personally that, in addition to being the Son of God, Jesus also became a human being?*

JESUS ANNOUNCES THAT HE IS THE MESSIAH (Luke 4:1-30)

*J*esus' ministry began near his home, but extended north to Capernaum after He was rejected in Nazareth.

1. (4:3,5-7,9-11) *In what categories of life did Satan try to tempt Christ?*

2. (4:4,8,12) *Why did Jesus reply to each of Satan's temptations with Scripture?*

3. (4:14-29) *It is interesting to note that these verses summarize the entire course of Jesus' ministry, ending in rejection and hatred. How did the people respond to Jesus at first (verse 15)?*

❒ *Why would they react this way?*

4. (4:16-24) *In the synagogue, Jesus read Isaiah 61:1-2 and then announced that He was the Messiah who had been prophesied. Why were those who heard Jesus speak astonished and skeptical?*

5. (4:25-27) *Why do you think Jesus used Gentiles—the widow in Sarepta (verse 26) and Naaman (verse 27)—to illustrate how God meets people's needs?*

6. (4:28-30) *Why did people from Jesus' hometown (Nazareth) respond to Him in anger?*

❒ *What are some of the responses you have observed in people today as they are confronted with who Jesus is and what He did?*

JESUS DEMONSTRATES THAT HE IS THE MESSIAH (Luke 4:31-44)

*I*n order to validate His claim as Messiah, Jesus demonstrated His power over demons and illness. He also began preaching in Judea.

1. (4:31-32) *What do you think the people meant when they said Jesus taught with power?*

2. (4:40-41) *While it was easy to say "I am the Messiah," Jesus proved His claim through His miraculous acts and His fulfillment of prophecy. In what two areas of life did Jesus demonstrate His authority?*

3. (4:33-35,41) *Why do you think Jesus made demons keep quiet when they knew who He was?*

4. (4:42-44) *What did the people want Jesus to do? Why?*

❑ *Why didn't He do what they wanted?*

❑ *How do you think Jesus felt as a result of the tension between the people's demands and His commitment?*

DIGGING DEEPER

1. *For a believer today, what does baptism signify?*

2. *What are some areas in which we might be tempted today that correspond to those general areas in which Satan tempted Jesus?*

❑ *What are some things we can do to resist these temptations?*

3. *How much do other people's responses affect your follow-through and obedience to God's direction in your life?*

❑ *In what ways could others' responses hinder your obedience to God?*

❑ *In what ways might others encourage you in obeying God?*

❖

Jesus' Call to Discipleship
LUKE 5—6

*R*ecently, a major corporation staged a gala extravaganza to unveil a new line of products. Hundreds of people in formal attire were amused by renowned entertainers. Guests sampled sumptuous cuisine, indulging themselves in delicacy after extravagant delicacy. And the sole purpose of this excess was to announce a line of mediocre products. Some suggested that the money spent on the reception could better have been spent on developing the product line! "Hype" is the name of the game! A store doesn't simply open and begin serving customers; it has a grand opening with games, prizes, and gifts galore!

The inauguration of a new leader, whether local, national, or head of state, is an occasion for celebration, festivities, and the grandeur of an elaborate ceremony. Such excess and elegance is not unique to our day. Throughout history, leaders have made sure that they were installed with due recognition.

But Jesus Christ was an exception. He began His ministry with no fanfare or recognition from the "beautiful people." Jesus announced His coming in the outdoors to the common folk—thronged by the deaf, the lame, and the blind. Some of his first followers were simple workers, dressed in clothes that reeked of fish and hard labor. As you study this passage, keep in mind who Christ actually was and the significance of what He was going to do. And contrast His inauguration with that of today's leaders.

JESUS' CALL OF PETER, JAMES, AND JOHN (Luke 5:1-11)

*T*his section begins with Jesus teaching great crowds by the Sea of Galilee, standing in the boat of Simon Peter. At Jesus' command Simon went out to deep water and caught a great number of fish. This event brought Simon Peter to his knees and the three left their fishing to follow Jesus.

1. (5:1-11) *Based on these verses, how would you describe Peter?*

2. (5:10-11) *Fishermen had little status, even though they were skilled workers. Why do you think that Christ chose common men—not wealthy, prestigious, famous, or powerful men—to assist Him?*

3. (5:11) *It was common for itinerant teachers to accumulate followers who would travel with them and learn from them. What personal sacrifices did Peter, James, and John make by following Christ?*

❒ *What sacrifices might people today be called upon to make in following Jesus?*

❒ *What sacrifices have you made to follow Jesus?*

4. (5:10,27, 6:12-16) *Obviously, there was great diversity among those whom Jesus called to follow Him. How should that challenge and encourage us today?*

JESUS' ANNOUNCEMENT TO THE PRIESTS (Luke 5:12-16)

*I*n these verses a leper pled with Jesus to heal him. After healing the leper with a touch, Jesus told him to go show himself to the priest (following the Law of Moses, for confirmation of the healing and to offer a sacrifice— Leviticus 14:1-20), and not to tell others. But news of the miracle spread rapidly.

1. (5:12) *How do you think the man with leprosy knew enough about Jesus to be able to have faith in His ability?*

2. (5:15) *How would you describe the general attitude and response of the people living in this region to Jesus?*

❏ *How did Jesus' fame and reputation affect Him?*

❏ *How do famous, high-visibility Christians today tend to respond to being well-known?*

3. (5:16) *What are some of the reasons that Jesus might have felt it was necessary for Him to get off alone to pray to His Father?*

❏ *Does public acclaim usually drive most people to solitude and prayer? Why or why not?*

JESUS' ANNOUNCEMENT TO THE SCRIBES AND PHARISEES (Luke 5:17—6:11)

*T*hese verses describe confrontations between Jesus and the scribes and Pharisees. They criticized almost every aspect of Jesus' ministry—forgiving sins, healing a paralytic, and attending a banquet given by Levi. They also criticized His eating habits, His disciples' picking grain on the Sabbath, and Jesus' healing on the Sabbath.

1. (5:22-24) *Jesus taught an important lesson after healing the man with palsy. What was the relationship between having authority to forgive sins and being able to heal the sick?*

2. (5:20-21,29-30,33, 6:1-2,7-8,10-11) *Rather than evaluating Jesus' ministry on the basis of the Old Testament prophecies concerning the Messiah, it appears that the religious leaders made up their minds before learning the facts. List the actions and attitudes found in this passage for which the religious leaders criticized Jesus.*

3. (5:21,30,33, 6:2,7,11) *Why do you think the leaders responded so negatively and so violently to the ministry of Jesus?*

4. (5:31-32) *What is the point of Jesus' statement that it is the sick, not the well (whole), who need a physician?*

5. (5:37-39) *Grape juice was sealed in new, flexible wineskins that expanded with fermentation. Old skins were brittle and would burst as the wine fermented. Building on the wine analogy, Pharisees preferred the old tradition to Jesus' new teaching. Many sincere religious leaders viewed habit and tradition as more important than Jesus' teaching. How do some people today demonstrate this same attitude?*

JESUS CALLS HIS TWELVE APOSTLES AND EXPLAINS GENUINE DISCIPLESHIP (Luke 6:12-49)

Verses 12-49 include Jesus' choice of the twelve men who became His apostles and Luke's summary of the extended passage we refer to as The Sermon on the Mount (Matthew 5—7). In this sermon, Jesus described God's expectations for a person living in His kingdom.

1. (6:20-38; see also Galatians 3:10-14; Romans 5:1) *Why would Jesus present a behavior standard that is humanly impossible to achieve?*

❏ *Alone, we cannot hope to achieve God's standard of righteousness explained in these verses. Read Romans 3:21-24 and summarize how we can be made righteous before God.*

2. (6:39-45) *What central theme ties together the illustrations of the blind guide, the critical brother, and the tree and fruit?*

3. (6:46-49) *A beautiful building with a weak foundation is useless. What people living in His time do you think Jesus was referring to when He gave the illustration of the man building on the rock and the man building on the sand?*

❑ *How would this illustration relate to people today?*

4. How do you think the disciples (including the twelve apostles) felt when Jesus finished this sermon?

DIGGING DEEPER

1. Peter, James, John, and Levi immediately left their vocations and followed Jesus (5:11,28). What are some things that Jesus might call you to leave behind in order to follow Him?

2. Jesus was sensitive and compassionate even to those such as the leper whom society rejected (5:12-13). List some ways that Christians today can follow His example.

3. Jesus wanted followers who would hear and do His sayings (6:47, cf. James 1:22-27, 2:14-20). Select one teaching of Jesus that you will apply in your life this week.

4. What are some "religious" things that we could do that might take the place of a personal relationship with Jesus Christ?

5. If you have already accepted Jesus' gift of righteousness, write a brief "thank-you" prayer here. If you haven't, why not write down and then pray a prayer accepting Jesus as your Saviour right now?

❖

The Beginning of Jesus' Ministry Around Capernaum
LUKE 7—8

*S*eeing is believing, at least according to the old adage. Many seem to feel that if only they could see something, they would be able to believe. But there are several obvious fallacies in this reasoning.

One fallacy is assuming that seeing something will convince us to change our minds. This really doesn't work too often. For instance, in the physical realm we know the consequence of two senses fighting each other. Anyone who has been seasick knows the power of that conflict. Our eyes tell us that we are sitting still, yet our inner ear (correctly) insists that we are moving. The conflict rages until finally our stomachs give the definitive answer!

The conflict can be even greater if what we see disagrees with our preconceived beliefs and ideas. A friend of ours explains it this way: "You can't extinguish an emotional fire with an ocean of logic." This was Jesus' experience, too. Many people had already decided to reject Him. In spite of all the evidence to the contrary, they would not accept that He was the Messiah. And so Jesus' ministry began with simultaneous acclaim and rejection— loved by the common folk, hated by the religious leaders.

JESUS AUTHENTICATES HIS MINISTRY (Luke 7:1-29)

*T*he scribes and Pharisees may have been all too willing to criticize Jesus and His works, but others dared to trust Him. These verses contain the account of Jesus healing a centurion's servant and raising the dead son of a widow from Nain. They also include the answer to John's question about whether or not Jesus was the Messiah.

1. (7:1-10) *Roman dominance over Israel was deeply resented by most Jews. It is remarkable that the centurion appears to have been highly respected by the people in this region. List the positive characteristics attributed to the centurion in these verses.*

❏ *What does this tell us about our lifestyles and how we can gain respect among those who do not hold our faith?*

2. (7:12-16) *Why did Jesus raise the widow's son from the dead?*

3. (7:16-17) *How did the common people seem to feel about Jesus during this early stage of His ministry?*

4. (7:22-23) *Apparently, John the Baptist had some questions about Jesus, perhaps wondering why he was still in prison if the Messiah had come. What evidence did Jesus offer to John's followers as proof that He was the Messiah?*

5. (7:27-35) *According to these verses, what was the relationship between John's ministry and Jesus' ministry?*

RELIGIOUS LEADERS REJECT JESUS
(Luke 7:30-50)

*M*ost of the wise and respected religious leaders rejected Jesus. But many of the common people accepted Him, including the woman with a bad reputation who anointed Jesus' feet.

1. (7:30-35) *Jesus likens those who rejected both John and Him to children (verse 32) who are unhappy with any alternatives. What lack of logic is apparent in the reasons the religious leaders rejected John and Jesus?*

2. (7:41-43) *What do you think was the point of Jesus' illustration about the two men who had their debts forgiven?*

33

3. (7:37-47) *Why was it presumptuous for Simon to criticize the woman as a sinner?*

❏ *In what way did the woman's attitude differ from the Pharisees' attitudes?*

❏ *How do we make presumptions about people and label them sinners?*

JESUS DESCRIBES VARIOUS RESPONSES TO HIS TEACHING (Luke 8:1-21)

*J*esus used the Parable of the Sower and the Soils to describe various responses to His teaching. This section concludes with Christ's affirmation that those who obey Him become His family.

1. (8:5-15) *Planting in ancient Israel was done by scattering seed by hand, so distribution was not carefully controlled. The seed could easily fall onto many different types of ground. In Jesus' parable, what are the four kinds of soil on which the seed fell and what do they signify?*

Soils   **People represented**

1.

2.

3.

4.

❒ If Jesus' words have taken root in the good soil of our own hearts, what kind of fruit should we be bearing?

2. (8:16-17) How does the illustration of a lamp on a stand relate to the good soil (verse 15) in the preceding parable?

3. (8:19-21) Jesus did not ignore His own family responsibility, rather He broadened "family" to include all believers. How should we relate to fellow Christians and what role should they play in our lives?

JESUS DEMONSTRATES POWER OVER NATURE, DEMONS, DEATH, AND ILLNESS (Luke 8:22-56)

*E*vidences of Christ's power included calming a storm, healing a demoniac, and healing a woman and Jairus' daughter. Only God could have done such things. They represented proof that the Son of God walked among them as the Son of Man.

1. (8:22-25) Violent storms often struck unexpectedly on the Sea of Galilee. The disciples, with oars, were no match for furious weather. Why were they amazed by what happened on the Sea of Galilee?

2. (8:34-37) A Roman legion was 6,000 men. Apparently, the demon's response indicated that many demons possessed this man simultaneously. Why do you think the people were not thankful that Jesus healed the demon-possessed man?

35

3. (8:38-39) *Why was the response of the healed man so different from the response of his neighbors?*

4. (8:44,48) *Even though the crowd was crushing Jesus, why do you think that only one woman was affected by touching His clothing?*

5. (8:41-42,53,56) *Compare the various responses to Jesus in these verses. What does each response indicate about that person's attitude toward Jesus?*

DIGGING DEEPER

1. *In Luke 7:6-8, the centurion recognizes Jesus' authority. How should we recognize and respond to Jesus' authority?*

❒ *How can we communicate this important truth with friends and acquaintances who do not recognize His authority?*

2. *Even though John the Baptist was great, those who would respond to Christ (becoming part of the kingdom of God) would have far greater privilege (7:28). In what sense do we, as Christians today, have greater roles and privileges than John did?*

3. *What are some of the ways in which Christians today provide light (8:16) to the world?*

☐ *What actions or attitudes in your life might cause the light of your witness to become "dim" to unbelievers who observe your life?*

4. *The woman in Luke 8:44 demonstrated her faith by touching Jesus. In what ways do you demonstrate your faith today?*

❖

"ACTUALLY, JESUS SENT US TO MINISTER TO OTHER PEOPLE, BUT HE CAN STAY IF HE'S QUIET."

What It Means to be a Disciple
LUKE 9—10

"**W**hom the Lord loveth He maketh rich!" Or at least it seems that's how many want to interpret Scripture.

There always have been those who would try to gain material profit from Christianity. In the past, though, this kind of activity was kept to a minimum, or at least it wasn't flaunted openly. But that has changed. Today there seems to be a never-ending stream of "wealth-and-prosperity" medicine men hawking their spiritual snake oil. Such charlatans would have us trade our crosses for pin-striped suits, and rewrite Luke 9:58: "Foxes have holes and birds of the air have nests, but the Son of man prefers five-star hotels."

Jesus flatly stated that it *costs* a person something to become His disciple. This kind of teaching is not very popular today. Rather, we are told that we can be, should be, and certainly deserve to be, wealthy. But as you read Luke 9 and 10, take a look at what Jesus really says about discipleship. His definition of wealth is vastly different from the lie promoted by Satan.

JESUS PREPARES AND SENDS OUT THE TWELVE (Luke 9:1-17)

*J*esus prepared the twelve disciples to go out and proclaim the exciting message that Messiah had come! After they returned, He demonstrated His power and compassion by feeding a multitude with five loaves and two fish.

1. (9:1-2) *According to these verses, why did Jesus send the apostles out? How did He empower them to fulfill the job He gave them to do?*

❏ *How has Jesus empowered you to fulfill your work for Him?*

2. (9:3-5) *The disciples carried a very important message about the Messiah. How were they instructed to receive support?*

❏ *Why would Jesus give them instructions about those who did not receive them?*

3. (9:11-17) *Why were the people so excited about Jesus at this point?*

☐ *How does a "wealth-and-prosperity" gospel become a trap similar to what these early followers of Jesus fell into?*

4. (9:13) *In the desert place, why did Jesus tell His disciples to provide food when it was obvious that they could not?*

5. (9:14-17) *Notice the details that indicate Jesus made sure the food was distributed in a systematic, orderly manner. What lessons do you see here for us today?*

JESUS CONFIRMS WHO HE IS
(Luke 9:18-36)

*J*esus explained what it meant to be a disciple, and the persecution we should expect. Then Jesus revealed a hint of His true glory on the Mount of Transfiguration.

1. (9:18-22) *Jesus had just sent His disciples out to many cities to proclaim the kingdom of God was here. Why would he command the disciples now, after feeding 5,000 people miraculously, not to tell anyone that He is the Messiah, the Christ of God?*

❏ What were some of the events that Jesus told His disciples would happen to Him?

2. (9:23-26) How did Jesus explain discipleship to His disciples? What did Jesus expect of His followers?

❏ How do these expectations directly contradict principles that many believe and live by today?

❏ How would you restate this test of discipleship in your words?

3. (9:33) At the transfiguration, Moses and Elijah represent the beginning of the law (Moses) and the end of Israel (Elijah) at the terrible "Day of the Lord" (Malachi 4:5-6). Why did Peter respond as he did?

❏ In what ways do some people today make the same mistake that Peter made in assuming that human religious leaders are equal to Jesus?

4. (9:34-35) What was God's response to Peter's idea?

THE DEMANDS OF DISCIPLESHIP
(Luke 9:37-62)

After healing a demon-possessed boy, Jesus explained both the source of greatness and the expectations of a disciple.

1. (9:44-45) *Why were the disciples confused by Jesus' teaching?*

2. (9:46-48) *When His disciples were seeking position and power, how did Jesus redefine greatness for them?*

❐ *How do you define greatness?*

3. (9:53) *Why did the Samaritans refuse to welcome Jesus?*

4. (9:54-56) *Jesus' disciples wanted retribution for the Samaritans' attitude but, according to Jesus, what should be our attitude toward those who reject or even oppose Him?*

5. (9:57-62) *List the reasons given here for not following Jesus, and Jesus' assessment of the attitudes represented.*

❏   What principles of discipleship for your life do you see in these verses?

JESUS SENDS OUT SEVENTY
(Luke 10:1-24)

*J*esus sent out His disciples (70 this time) to prepare people for the Messiah and received reports on their return.

1. (10:1-12) *Jesus commanded that they pray for workers, and yet it seemed that they were to be the workers. How do praying for something and being part of the answer fit together?*

❏   *Why do you think Jesus sent them out in pairs?*

❏   *What does that say to us about our service?*

❏   *Why did He call them lambs among wolves?*

❏   *What does that say to us about our service?*

2. (10:17-21) *What might the 70 disciples have rejoiced over, and what did Jesus say is more valuable?*

❏ *What symbols or positions might we inappropriately view as more important than our relationship with Christ Himself?*

JESUS EXPLAINS HIS VALUE SYSTEM (Luke 10:25-41)

*J*esus used the Parable of the Good Samaritan to teach us important truths about love and how to relate to others. Then He stressed the importance of not becoming too busy to do good things.

1. (10:25,29) *A lawyer was a Pharisee who specialized in studying the details of the Mosaic law and the Pharisees' interpretation of it. Why did this lawyer come to Jesus to ask Him these questions?*

2. (10:33) *The Samaritans and the Jews had a long-standing animosity. Why do you think Jesus made a Samaritan the hero of this parable?* ›

❏ *What principles for our lives can we draw from the Parable of the Good Samaritan?*

3. (10:37) *What do you think the lawyer felt as he left Jesus?*

4. (10:39-42) *When Jesus came to her home, what common trap did Martha fall into?*

❏ *What principles of Christ-like living can you draw from this situation in the lives of Mary and Martha?*

DIGGING DEEPER

1. *What are some things that Jesus might call us to do that seem impossible without His power and provision?*

❏ *Why would He do that?*

2. *What things might Christians today do that non-Christians would say would be wasting or "losing" our lives?*

❏ *Is there anything in your life today that Jesus wants you to give up in order to follow Him?*

3. *What types of people might you have a hard time accepting and caring about?*

❐ *Why?*

❐ *What actions can you take to demonstrate acceptance of others and humility, the true marks of Christ-like greatness:*

—at home?

—at work?

—in your church?

—in your neighborhood?

4. *In what situations might you fall into the same trap as Martha?*

❐ *How can you avoid this and cultivate an attentiveness like Mary's?*

❖

6

"I'M WAITING FOR JESUS TO RETURN. WHAT ARE YOU WAITING FOR?"

Jesus Prepares His Followers
LUKE 11:1—13:21

*G*etting ready for a cross-country move is a major undertaking. Before we moved several years ago, we spent weeks packing up and preparing our home for occupancy by the new family. And, as we approached closing, we felt that we had done a pretty good job.

But certain things could only be done just prior to leaving. During the final "walk through" with the new owner, we had many things to explain. The new family needed to know details about the heating and air-conditioning systems. The appliances had written instructions, but we wanted to pass along little tips that we had gleaned over the years. We especially wanted to explain about the central vacuum that we had installed, along with the electronic air filter, the humidifier, and the wood burning stove.

There was also specific information about the landscaping. Certain of the shrubs and perennials needed special care. We told the family about the fruit trees, the evergreens, and other gardening features. And since we needed to communicate more than the new owners could absorb, we wrote down much of the information so that they could refer back to what they had had verbally explained.

What we did prior to our moving date was similar to what Jesus did with His disciples. Not only did Jesus teach, preach, and heal the sick, but He also was preparing His disciples to carry on the ministry after He was gone. Even as we instructed our home's new owners, Jesus assigned various tasks to His disciples. And always there were warnings. This passage includes many of those warnings Jesus gave His disciples.

INSTRUCTIONS FOR PRAYING
(Luke 11:1-13)

*C*ommunicating with our holy God is an awesome privilege. Jesus taught His disciples to pray and encouraged them—and us!—with assurance of God's loving answers.

1. **(11:2-4)** *What are the five requests that Jesus included in His prayer? (This account gives less detail than the parallel passage in Matthew 6:9-15.)*

❐ *Do we frequently omit any of these five areas in our praying? If so, why?*

❏ *What should you include more of in your prayer life if you want to follow Jesus' example?*

2. (11:9-13) *What do these verses suggest about how God responds to requests from us?*

❏ *How is the Holy Spirit (verse 13) one "good gift" from God the Father to us?*

WARNING ABOUT SPIRITUAL FORCES
(Luke 11:14-36)

When Jesus cast out demons, some claimed it was by Satan's power. Jesus warned them about spiritual insensitivity and impending judgment.

1. (11:15) *What did some of the religious leaders want people to think about Jesus' ability to cast out demons?*

❏ *Why would they do this?*

2. (11:24-26) *What do you think Jesus meant when He emphasized that just getting rid of evil is not enough?*

3. (11:29-32) *What parallels can you think of between Jonah (Jonas) and Jesus?*

❐ *Even the Queen of Sheba (verse 31) and the Ninevites (verse 32), who were heathens, responded to God's revelation. How did their response condemn unbelieving Jews of Jesus' day?*

❐ *What does it say about people today?*

❐ *How could you use this in witnessing?*

4. (11:34-36) *What do you think that Jesus was warning about when He emphasized the importance of the "eye"?*

❐ *How can the input that we receive through our eyes influence our lives?*

WARNINGS TO RELIGIOUS LEADERS
(Luke 11:37-54)

*J*esus strongly warned the religious leaders who were leading the people astray. The same kind of evil influence is alive and prospering today. There are key truths for us in this passage, too.

1. (11:37-41) *What did the Pharisees seem most concerned about and what concerned Jesus?*

❏ *A lawyer, or scribe, was an authority on the detailed regulations of the Law which covered every area of life. But these men often were more concerned with the letter than the spirit of the law. In what ways can worry preoccupy our lives so that we fail to do what we should?*

2. (11:42-52) *What were the six reasons why Jesus pronounced woe (i.e., condemnation) on the Pharisees?*

❏ *Why might Jesus pronounce woe on this nation today?*

ENCOURAGEMENT TO FAITHFULNESS
(Luke 12:1-12)

*J*esus warned His disciples that those things done in private will someday be made known. His serious warning against ignoring the Holy Spirit should speak to our hearts as well.

1. **(12:1-3)** *Leaven (yeast) is something that is not seen; it works "under cover" to produce results. Here Jesus used it to symbolize the hypocrisy of the Pharisees. In what ways could we fall prey to hypocritical attitudes similar to those of the Pharisees?*

2. **(12:4-7)** *When persecution comes, how should it help us to understand that God knows everything about us?*

3. **(12:8-10)** *What is the relationship between a person's attitude toward Jesus and the Holy Spirit, and how God responds to that person?*

4. **(12:11-12)** *When would the disciples need the guidance of the Holy Spirit under persecution?*

❑ *Why would we?*

ENCOURAGEMENT TO SPIRITUAL VALUES
(Luke 12:13-34)

*J*esus taught that spiritual values take precedence over material things, and that if people seek God first, He will take care of those things for His children.

1. (12:15,21-24) *What will preoccupation with physical things produce in terms of spiritual values?*

❏ *Make a list of the earthly treasures you value and the spiritual treasures you either have or want to have in Heaven. Which occupies most of your thoughts—honestly?*

Earthly Treasures   **Heavenly Treasures**

2. (12:16-19) *Why did the rich man feel so self-sufficient and complacent?*

3. (12:25-32) *Why did Jesus teach that people should not worry?*

❏ *What is the antidote to worry according to verse 31?*

4. (12:34) *What do you think Jesus meant when He said that our hearts will be where our treasures are?*

ENCOURAGEMENT TO BE PREPARED
(Luke 12:35-53)

An awareness of future things and the conflict that inevitably will come should produce an alert watchfulness and encourage careful preparation. How prepared are you?

1. (12:35-40) *From this first parable, what do you think Jesus wanted His disciples to do?*

2. (12:37-38) *What does Jesus suggest will be the reward for these disciples?*

3. (12:41-48) *Peter's question in verse 41 bridges the two parables. Jesus' exhortation to His disciples was different from what follows directed to the Jewish religious leaders. Based on Jesus' comments leading up to verses 42-48, what did the Jewish religious leaders fail to do?*

4. (12:47-48) *Who were those who should have known the master's will and who were entrusted with much?*

❐ *With what were they entrusted?*

❏ *In light of what God entrusts to us, how does this second parable apply today?*

FINAL REJECTION BY THE JEWISH LEADERS (Luke 12:54—13:21)

*J*esus related that the Jewish leaders could not discern the times. He used the Parable of the Gardener and the healing of a woman on the Sabbath to confirm the Jews' rejection.

1. (12:54-59)   *It is ironic that the people were more skilled at interpreting physical signs (about the weather) than spiritual. In what areas of life should these people have been judging themselves?*

2. (13:10-16)   *This is the last time Jesus preached in the synagogue. It signals the final rejection by the Jewish leaders. What reasons did Jesus give to justify breaking pharisaic tradition by healing on the Sabbath?*

3. (13:17)   *Why do you think Jesus' opponents were humiliated (ashamed)?*

❏ *What glorious things made the people rejoice?*

❒ Why do you think from this point Jesus turned from the Jewish leaders and took His message to everyone?

DIGGING DEEPER

1. What difference would it make in your life this week if you really believed and remembered that every thought and action would become known (12:2-3)?

2. What are some actions we can take to keep our possessions in proper perspective?

❒ What should you be doing to lay up treasures that can't be lost?

3. What are some things we can do to be prepared and watchful for the coming of the Son of Man (12:35-40)?

7

"IS IT ALL RIGHT TO LOVE YOUR MATERIAL POSSESSIONS IF THEY LOVE YOU BACK?"

The True Nature of God's Kingdom
LUKE 13:22—16:31

*T*elevision commercials can be fascinating. Some people even prefer commercials to the shows themselves. One of the values of commercials (other than the obvious sales benefits) is that they provide peepholes into the mind of a nation. Real national values show through in commercials. For instance, we discover the horror and shame of being caught with collar stains; we find that people who perspire are scorned and avoided. Commercials tell us that if we wear what the stars wear, drink the athletes' drink, use the make-up of the beautiful people, and drive the car that says we have arrived, others will know we are *somebody*.

Unfortunately, these ideas are not unique to our time or culture. In New Testament times, Pharisees constantly pretended to be something that they weren't. When Jesus confronted them, revealing their hypocrisy, they hated Him. And so they rejected Him and tried to influence the entire nation to follow them. This section describes the culmination of the religious leaders' rejection of Jesus, and Jesus' redirection of ministry.

JESUS' SORROW OVER REJECTION
(Luke 13:22—14:14)

Jesus taught that it is hard to get into the kingdom, and sorrowed over Jerusalem for rejecting Him. Then, He confronted the Pharisees with their rejection, and the hypocrisy it revealed.

1. (13:34-35) *What did Jesus want to do for the Jewish nation, and how did they respond to Him and to the prophets?*

2. (14:3-6) *What was Jesus really asking the Pharisees and what was the result?*

3. (14:11) *This verse presents a basic principle of the kingdom of God. What is it?*

❐ *How can you put this into practice in your daily life:*

— at home?

— at work?

— at church?

4. (14:12-14) *Why would one of the best ways to demonstrate true spirituality be to give to those who cannot repay our kindness...or to those who do not know it is our kindness?*

GUIDELINES FOR GOD'S KINGDOM
(Luke 14:15-35)

Jesus uses another parable to teach His disciples. This time He describes a banquet where the invited guests refused to come, so others were invited. He then warned His followers to count the cost of discipleship.

1. (14:18-20,24) *Jesus likened the kingdom of God to a feast. In the application of the parable, who is represented by the ones invited to the feast but would not come?*

2. (14:21,23) *Whom do the alternates invited as replacements represent?*

3. (14:26-27) *Jesus was not suggesting that His followers neglect responsibility, merely that earthly relationships cannot take precedence over discipleship. What were some of the costs that the disciples had to pay for following Jesus?*

❑ *What costs might we have to pay to follow Jesus?*

4. (14:28-35) *What principles for Christian living do you think Jesus was teaching in these three parables?*

5. (14:33) *What did Jesus mean when He said that His disciples had to give up everything?*

GOD'S CONCERN FOR SEEKING THE LOST (Luke 15:1-32)

*T*his section includes three of Jesus' best known parables—the Lost Sheep, the Lost Coin, and the Prodigal Son. Each teaches us how Jesus views those who are not His followers.

1. (15:1-10) *What do the Parables of the Lost Sheep and the Lost Coin tell us about how God views individuals?*

2. (15:12) *In the third parable, why do you think the father gave the son what he requested even though the father knew it would not be best?*

3. (15:14-20) *What were some of the reasons why the younger son repented?*

4. (15:20-32) *In this parable, the older brother probably represents the Pharisees (who served out of duty) and the younger brother represents true disciples (who serve out of love). How do the attitudes of the older brother and the father differ toward the prodigal?*

THE PLACE OF WEALTH IN THE KINGDOM (Luke 16:1-31)

*C*hrist's exhortation on attitudes toward money and the abuse of wealth is clear in the account of the rich man and Lazarus.

1. (16:1-9) *Jesus is not commending dishonesty. He is saying that the ungodly should look to the future and so should the godly. How did the unjust manager plan ahead?*

❐ *Why did the rich man commend the steward's actions (verse 8)?*

2. (16:10) *What principle of trustworthiness does Jesus teach here?*

3. (16:13) *Jesus did not criticize having or using money. He does condemn allowing it to dominate or control one's life. What would be the difference in the way a person would act if he were serving God or serving money?*

Serving God   **Serving Money**

4. (16:19-31) *In what sense did the rich man and Lazarus exchange places after their deaths?*

❐ *What single life truth would you derive from this passage?*

DIGGING DEEPER

1. *In light of Jesus' response toward those who rejected Him, how should we feel, and how should we act toward those who hate and reject Him?*

—Toward those who hate and reject us because we love and serve Jesus?

2. *What costs should we consider if we really want to be disciples of Jesus Christ?*

3. *What principles do you find in James 4:6-10 that would help you have a Christ-honoring attitude toward yourself and others?*

4. In what areas of your life do you need to be more faithful to God (e.g., money, time, possessions)?

❏ What steps will you take to develop faithfulness?

❖

8

"A RAINY DAY! JUST WHAT WE'VE BEEN SAVING FOR!"

Jesus' Teaching on Kingdom Living
LUKE 17:1—19:27

*A*ll of us have experienced the trauma that accompanies major changes in life. A change usually means breaking old habit patterns and establishing new ones. Certainly change brings new experiences that may force us to reevaluate beliefs and assumptions.

Ordinarily, major changes occur when a young person leaves home to attend college, to serve in the armed forces, to get an apartment, or to start a new job. These major transitions in life can be traumatic for the parents, too! Later on in life, changing jobs or moving also requires re-evaluation of routines and assumptions that govern daily life.

Marriage is another key turning point, bringing new experiences and forcing us to change habit patterns. It is difficult to begin thinking "we" not "I," and to look for ways to serve and encourage another rather than ourselves. However, once the transition has been made, it is just as traumatic to revert to a single lifestyle.

But those changes or transitions are all relatively minor compared with the ways that we must shift our thinking when we enter the kingdom of God at salvation. Jesus spent a great deal of His three years of ministry teaching expectations of kingdom living in contrast to what His followers had known. He who would save his life must lose it; it is more blessed to give than to receive; greatness comes through humiliation and service. This passage deals with the transition from focus on the earthly kingdom to the spiritual kingdom of God, and the changes that must accompany that transition.

TEACHING ON FAITH AND ATTITUDES (Luke 17:1-19)

*T*hese verses teach us about our attitudes toward sin and forgiveness, faith, duty, and giving thanks.

1. (17:1-6) *What makes it so difficult to apply the teaching in these verses about offending others, especially those most vulnerable (little ones)?*

❏ *What makes it so difficult to apply Jesus' instruction about forgiving others?*

2. (17:9-10) *What did Jesus teach about the proper attitude toward obligations?*

3. (17:15-19)   *What are the main truths of Jesus' statements when only one of the lepers returned?*

TEACHING ABOUT THE COMING KINGDOM (Luke 17:20-37)

*J*esus knew His disciples expected an earthly kingdom and failed to understand the spiritual kingdom He came to give. So He described the nature of the spiritual kingdom of God and explained how the physical, earthly kingdom will begin.

1. (17:20-21)   *What is the nature of the present, spiritual kingdom of God and how is it different from what the Jews expected?*

2. (17:22-37)   *These verses shift to when the future, earthly, Millennial kingdom will be established. What kinds of things (verses 26-29) cause people to be so preoccupied that they miss spiritual truths?*

❐ *Verses 26-35 describe the beginning of the Millennium (not the Rapture). What is the basic spiritual principle of life found in verse 33?*

TEACHING ABOUT ATTITUDES IN THE KINGDOM (Luke 18:1-34)

*T*o illustrate attitudes in the kingdom, Jesus told the Parables of the Widow, the Unjust Judge, and the Pharisee and the Tax Collector. Then He gave instructions about the proper attitudes toward children and riches. Finally, Jesus again forewarned His disciples of His death.

1. **(18:6-8)** *In what ways is God similar to the city judge?*

❐ *In what ways is He dissimilar?*

2. **(18:10-14)** *How are the differing attitudes of the Pharisee and tax collector sometimes seen in people today?*

3. **(18:17)** *The disciples viewed the children as bothering Jesus, but He used the children as an example of a proper response to spiritual teaching. What is the essential requirement for becoming a part of God's kingdom?*

❐ *What does this mean?*

4. (18:22-23) *What did the rich man's response indicate about his heart attitude toward God and his riches?*

5. (18:31-34, cf. John 14:26) *Why do you think the disciples could not understand Jesus' teaching about His coming death?*

EXAMPLES OF RESPONDING TO JESUS (Luke 18:35—19:10)

*J*esus showed how the Jews should have responded through the attitudes of the blind beggar and Zacchaeus.

1. (18:42) *What was the basis for the blind man's receiving his sight?*

2. (18:43) *What was the response of the observers, and why do you think that the people responded this way?*

3. (19:8) *Tax collectors were permitted to add their own fees (virtually, whatever amount they thought they could collect) to the taxes they received. After meeting Jesus, what was Zacchaeus's response and what did this indicate about his heart attitude?*

❏ *What principles can be drawn from Zaccheus's example about repaying those whom we have wronged?*

TEACHING ABOUT STEWARDSHIP (Luke 19:11-27)

*I*n the Parable of the Ten Pounds Jesus explains how those in His kingdom should view responsibility.

1. **(19:12)** *In this kingdom parable, the servants represent Jesus' followers, the subjects represent the nation of Israel, and the pounds represent opportunities to serve God. Whom do you think the nobleman in the parable represented?*

2. **(19:16-19)** *What is the relationship between the pounds earned and the reward given?*

3. **(19:24)** *Why do you think the servant who did nothing with what he was given was judged so harshly?*

DIGGING DEEPER

1. *What are some things that you tend to take for granted (as the nine lepers did) for which you should thank God?*

2. *What are some things that hinder you or get in your way of serving God?*

3. *What is your attitude toward money? What steps can you take to insure that you will keep or develop a proper attitude toward money?*

4. *Read I Timothy 6:17-19. What material resources has God given to you, and how might you invest them more wisely to receive eternal spiritual dividends?*

❖

"YES, SON. JESUS RODE INTO JERUSALEM ON A DONKEY, BUT JESUS WAS NOT A DEMOCRAT."

Jesus' Announcement as Messiah
LUKE 19:28—21:38

*P*eriodically, individuals predict that the end of the world is approaching. Some even advocate abandoning normal activities and responsibilities in order to prepare for the climactic events. Some years ago a group of people sold everything, donned white robes, and retired to a mountaintop to await Jesus' return. Needless to say, they were disappointed. Such individuals prove the proverb, "It is very difficult to prophesy, especially in regard to the future."

But there is another kind of prediction. Some people are keen observers of trends. These people see things that are happening and extend their consequences into the future. If they understand accurately what is happening, and are able to extrapolate appropriately, they may very well anticipate coming circumstances.

Both types of "prediction" are found in this passage. At the beginning of the passage, Jesus fulfills several of the biblical prophecies concerning the Messiah given by God through the prophets. Since these prophecies did not originate with fallible humans, they were fulfilled in precise detail.

And, yet, Jesus also refers to the importance of good insight. Jesus admonished His followers to be keenly aware of what is happening. Each believer should be awake and alert, ready to recognize events and trends as they occur. In so doing, we will be prepared for whatever comes.

JESUS ENTERS JERUSALEM IN TRIUMPH (Luke 19:28-48)

As Jesus entered Jerusalem just days before His death, He allowed His disciples to acclaim Him as the Messiah. He also sorrowed over Jerusalem, went to the temple, and cast out the merchants who had made a mockery of the worship and honor due His Father.

1. (19:35,38) *Read Zechariah 9:9 and Psalm 118:26. In what ways are these prophecies fulfilled during the events surrounding Jesus' triumphal entry into Jerusalem?*

2. (19:37-39) *Why do you think the Pharisees wanted Jesus to stop His followers from praising Him and giving Him acclaim?*

3. (19:41-44) *List several reasons why Jesus was moved to weep over Jerusalem.*

4. (19:47-48) *After Jesus cast out the merchants defiling the temple, what were the two different responses to His preaching?*

LEADERS ATTEMPT TO TRAP JESUS
(Luke 20:1—21:4)

*J*esus confronted the religious leaders over His authority, paying taxes, and questions concerning the resurrection. It is obvious that they have rejected Him and the revelation that He is the Messiah.

1. (20:3-6) *The chief priests (mainly Sadducees), the teachers of the law (mostly Pharisees), and the elders (laymen) were plotting together to trap Jesus. Why was it so hard for the religious leaders to answer the question Jesus asked about John's baptism?*

2. (20:9-16) *Based on what we have observed of Israel's response to God, who do the following people represent in the Parable of the Husbandman?*

the vineyard owner (lord)—

the servants—

the son—

the husbandmen—

3. (20:21-26) *When questioned about taxes, how did Jesus answer, and what was the response of the ones trying to trap Him?*

☐ *What does Jesus' teaching in this passage mean to you?*

4. (20:27-38) *Sadducees were an aristocratic group (mostly priests) who didn't believe in life after death, and so devised this preposterous account to trap Jesus. How did Jesus answer their question about the resurrection?*

5. (20:39-44) *What was the point of Jesus' question in verse 44 asking why David called one of his descendants "Lord"?*

6. (20:45—21:4) *In what ways do the attitudes of the scribes differ from the attitude of the poor widow?*

❐   *What lessons can we learn from this account about our attitudes as we serve Jesus today?*

JESUS TEACHES ABOUT THE END TIMES (Luke 21:5-38)

*T*his part of Jesus' teaching, called the Olivet Discourse, describes the events leading up to the Tribulation and Christ's return, with a parenthetical prediction of the disciples' experience before the destruction of Jerusalem in A.D. 70.

1. (21:7)   *What two questions did the disciples ask about coming events?*

❐   *Why do you think they asked Jesus these questions?*

2. (21:16,18)   *How could the statement in verse 16, "you shall they cause to be put to death," and the statement in verse 18, "there shall not an hair of your head perish," both be true?*

3. (21:22,24)   *According to Jesus, why was Jerusalem going to be trodden down? What does this mean?*

4. (21:27) *How will Christ's second coming appearance be different from His first?*

5. (21:34-36) *"This generation" (verse 32) probably refers to those who see the signs that precede Christ's return. What are Jesus' disciples to do as they await His return?*

DIGGING DEEPER

1. *What actions can we take today to show Jesus' position as our Lord and King and offer praise to Him?*

2. *How can we be sure that we keep our responsibilities to government and to God in balance?*

❏ *What obligations and expectations present a potential problem for Christians in our century?*

3. *How should Jesus' promise to guide our response to persecution (21:13-19) affect our attitudes and our actions?*

❖

The Last Supper and Jesus' Arrest
LUKE 22:1-62

*R*eliability seems to be the buzzword for American manufacturers today. Unfortunately, it's far easier to *talk* about reliability than to *be* reliable. And even though we are well aware of possible discrepancies between what a producer says and does, we still feel that we should be able to rely on manufacturers' promises.

Perhaps that is why it's so disappointing when a product or its manufacturer fail to measure up to our expectations. But it is far worse when a friend or relative lets us down. Many of us are skeptical of claims for products or services, but we still expect to find that important quality of reliability in our interpersonal relationships. If a friend agrees to do something for us, we feel that friend should follow through.

Most of the time we can depend on others, especially those with whom we have built close relationships. But in Jesus' moment of deepest need He found that those whom He had lived with and ministered to—those who loved and walked with Him—failed Him when He needed them most. In the moments of His life just before His arrest, Jesus found that His three closest friends could not watch and pray with Him. Jesus was so alone and forsaken that God sent an angel to minister to Him.

And that was only the beginning. Shortly after the Last Supper, one of His "friends" betrayed Him to the religious leaders for trial. Then another publicly denied that he knew Him. When Jesus descended into the valley of the shadow of death, He was alone—forsaken and abandoned.

JUDAS'S AGREEMENT TO BETRAY JESUS (Luke 22:1-6)

*F*or three years he had traveled with Jesus, sat under His teaching, and had been sent out to minister for Jesus. But prior to the Passover supper, Judas went to the chief priests and agreed to betray Jesus for a price.

1. (22:2) *At Passover the Jews celebrated their escape from Egypt under Moses and the deliverance of their firstborn from the death angel. What did the chief priests and the teachers want to do and why?*

2. (22:3-6) *Why do you think Judas betrayed Jesus?*

❒ *List several reasons why Jesus might have chosen Judas to follow Him, even though He knew Judas would betray Him.*

❐ *Based on Jesus' example, how should we treat someone who has betrayed our trust?*

JESUS' LAST SUPPER WITH HIS APOSTLES (Luke 22:7-38)

*L*uke records a detailed account of the preparation for the Last Supper, their last meal together, and Jesus' conversation with the apostles after supper.

1. (22:7, cf. John 1:29) *What is the significance of Jesus' death coinciding with the Jews' sacrifice of the Passover lamb?*

2. (22:14-16,18) *What was the relationship between Jesus' eating and drinking and the kingdom of God?*

3. (22:19-20) *This observance, initiated by Christ, is the basis for the ceremonial meal celebrated in the early church. This meal is the basis for our observance of Communion or the Lord's Supper. How did the bread and cup symbolize what Jesus was going to do?*

4. (22:24) *Why would the apostles have been arguing about greatness at a time like this?*

5. (22:25-27) *What basic attitudes are necessary for greatness in the kingdom of God? (See also Jesus' example of a servant's attitude in John 13:4-17.)*

❑ How do these "kingdom attitudes" contrast with "Gentile attitudes"?

6. (22:30-32,34-35) How do you think Peter felt when Jesus was talking to him?

7. (22:33) What mistake do you think Peter made when he expressed his readiness to die for Christ?

❑ How might this serve as a warning to us today?

JESUS PRAYS ON THE MOUNT OF OLIVES (Luke 22:39-46)

*F*ollowing the Last Supper, Jesus took several of His apostles with Him and went out to the Mount of Olives to pray.

1. (22:40,46) What kind of temptation do you think Jesus meant?

2. (22:42) Even though, in His humanity, Jesus dreaded what He was going to face, He submitted His personal preference to the will of God. What was the "cup" that Jesus would have preferred not to drink?

❑ Why do you think He was willing to drink it?

3. (22:45) *Why do you think Jesus' companions were exhausted from sorrow?*

JESUS' ARREST AND PETER'S DENIAL
(Luke 22:47-62)

*J*esus' arrest was a traumatic experience for His disciples, leading to Peter's repeated denial of his Lord.

1. (22:49-50) *How did some of the disciples expect to respond to the soldiers in the garden?*

2. (22:52-53) *What was the significance of Jesus' comments that there was no need to come after Him as one might seek to capture a thief?*

3. (22:57-60) *Why do you think Peter so vehemently denied knowing Jesus?*

❐ *Have you ever denied Jesus? How?*

4. (22:61-62) *How did Peter feel when Jesus looked at him?*

❐ *Contrast Peter's actions here with the day of Pentecost after the Holy Spirit had come upon him and the other apostles (Acts 2:14-36).*

❐   *What changed him?*

DIGGING DEEPER

1. *List Paul's specific commands from Philippians 2:5-11 that relate to Christ-like attitudes and achieving true greatness.*

Verse   **_Commands_**

❐   *How well do you fulfill them?*

2. *What steps can you take to make it easier to submit to God's will even when you don't feel like it?*

3. *When might you be tempted to feel presumptuous about your abilities to stand strong for Jesus?*

❐   *Who in the Bible is a good example of standing strong in adversity? Why were they able to do this?*

11

Jesus Accomplishes His Mission
LUKE 22:63—23:56

When the going gets tough, the tough get going.

This is how some presidents, professional athletes, and business executives like to think of themselves. And who wouldn't be enamored by the concept that the very best that we have in us will be brought out by adversity? All of us would like to think we have a depth of character and inner strength that will emerge when called out by crisis. We feel sure that in a moment of crisis we will be a tower of strength, a pillar of steel, and a refuge for innocent children, frightened women, and terrified men.

But is that so? Would we really rise to the occasion? Or would the tower crumble—the steel be rusty? Would we provide refuge or would we join the masses desperately seeking a protector? And perhaps most disconcerting, we are not even sure how to prepare ourselves for an emergency. We are sobered by the realization that historians alone will make the judgment on our reaction.

As Jesus neared the end of His ministry on earth, the drama of redemption was drawing to a climax. And in this climax, Jesus revealed unmistakably what kind of man He was. Walking to His execution, He comforted His mourners. On the very threshold of death, He spoke words of hope to the one sharing His fate. And through pain, humiliation, and rejection, He emerged as Jesus, the Christ—Son of Man, Son of God.

THE TRIAL OF JESUS (Luke 22:63—23:25)

After His arrest, the religious leaders determined Jesus must die. So He was tried by Pilate, sent to Herod, and then sent back to Pilate for final sentencing.

1. (22:63-65) *What did the soldiers demand Jesus do to prove His identity to them? What is their attitude?*

2. (22:66-71) *The elders or Sanhedrin (also called the Council of Seventy) were priests and religious law specialists. What was the conclusion of this council about who Jesus claimed to be? What is their attitude?*

3. (23:2) *What were the accusations against Jesus? Which was true?*

4. (23:4-7)   *Pilate was the Roman governor of Jerusalem under King Herod (a Jew) who had been appointed by the Emperor to govern Palestine. Why did Pilate send Jesus to Herod, even though Pilate found no fault in Him?*

5. (23:8-9)   *What seemed to be Herod's main interest in Jesus, and why do you think Jesus didn't answer him at all?*

6. (23:12-25)   *Why did Pilate condemn Jesus after finding Him faultless and release Barabbas instead?*

❏   *What is the significance of verse 12 in this scenario?*

THE CRUCIFIXION OF JESUS (Luke 23:26-43)

*O*n His way to the cross, Jesus warned the mourners of coming tribulation. As He suffered on the cross Jesus encouraged the repentant thief while the unrepentant thief mocked and scorned Him.

1. (23:27-28)   *Why do you think Jesus' followers were mourning?*

2. (23:29-30)   *Because Israel rejected the Messiah, they will suffer the Great Tribulation described in Revelation. What did*

Jesus' warning mean about those who never had borne children being more blessed than those who had?

3. (23:35-42) List those who communicated with Jesus while He was on the cross. What do their comments indicate about their heart attitudes?

Person	_Comment_	_Attitude_

4. (23:34-43) How did Jesus respond to those around Him?

THE DEATH OF JESUS
(Luke 23:44-49)

As Jesus died, the world changed. The sky grew dark and the veil of the temple tore from top to bottom. Jesus released His spirit, and the centurion confessed God, while Jesus' followers watched from afar.

1. (23:44-45) Why do you think that God caused it to become dark from noon until 3:00 p.m.?

2. (23:45) The veil was a heavy fabric curtain in the temple separating the people from God's presence in the holy of holies. What is the significance of the veil being torn in two from top to bottom at the moment Jesus died?

3. (23:46) *What does Jesus' statement committing His spirit to God indicate about who was in control? (See also John 10:17-18.)*

4. (23:47-49) *What were the responses of those who watched Jesus die?*

<u>**Watchers**</u>   <u>**Response**</u>

the centurion

the people

*Jesus' followers
and acquaintances*

THE BURIAL OF JESUS
(Luke 23:50-56)

*F*ollowing Jesus' death, Joseph of Arimathea took the body of Jesus and placed it in a tomb while the women prepared spices for the body.

1. (23:50-52) *This council was the Sanhedrin, the group that demanded Jesus' death. What do these verses indicate about Joseph of Arimathea's character?*

❏ *What dangers might Joseph have risked in asking for Jesus' body?*

❏ *How does the example of Joseph warn us not to generalize about all people in a certain group?*

2. (23:55-56) *How do you think the women felt on the evening and the day following Jesus' death?*

❏ *How do you feel during a communion service or a Good Friday service when you think of Jesus' death? What does it mean to you?*

DIGGING DEEPER

1. *In what ways do people today respond to Jesus as either Pilate or Herod did?*

2. *What examples do we find for ourselves as we observe the way Jesus accepted ill-treatment?*

3. *Jesus' death gave us direct access to God. What steps will you take this week to take greater advantage of your accessibility to God?*

4. *Look at Hebrews 9, especially verses 24-28. List the differences between Old Testament blood sacrifices (in the tabernacle and temple) and Christ's sacrificial death.*

Tabernacle/Temple   **Christ's Sacrifice**

❖

12

"I WANT TO BE AN OBEDIENT CHRISTIAN, BUT THE DISOBEDIENT CHILD KEEPS GETTING IN THE WAY."

Jesus Completes His Earthly Ministry
LUKE 15:21—16:20

*R*ecently, we were eating dinner in a restaurant. Since we really did not need it, we had decided to forego dessert. But that was before the waitress, with calculated strategy, brought around the dessert tray. She tempted our palates, presenting item after luscious item, described in the most enticing manner possible.

And we succumbed! When the delicacies arrived, we knew that however many calories it cost, the price was well worth it. With taste buds poised in anticipation, Wes gently savored the first bite. But what a disappointment! Without a doubt, that was one of the worst desserts that we have ever eaten. Perhaps part of our problem was the visual appeal and the waitress's elaborate description. It may be that nothing could have measured up to that introduction. But whatever the reason, we had been oversold badly—promised more than was delivered.

We often meet people who oversell themselves or their products. But not Jesus. When Jesus lived among men, He never oversold Himself. What He said, He did. And, in fact, delivered far more to those who took Him at His word than they ever anticipated. Following His resurrection, Jesus met with His disciples and reviewed the things He had told them. And He explained some future events—things that they could be sure of because Jesus never oversold.

JESUS RISES FROM THE DEAD
(Luke 24:1-12)

*T*he day of the resurrection, the women went to the tomb and met two "men" who explained that Jesus had risen. The women remembered Jesus' words and ran to tell the disciples who could not believe it. Peter went to see for himself.

1. **(24:1-7)** *List the dramatic events described here.*

2. **(24:8)** *Jesus' teaching about His crucifixion and resurrection is recorded in Luke 9:31 and 18:31-34. Why do you think it took this long for Jesus' followers to remember what Jesus had taught them earlier?*

3. (24:11) *How was the resurrection announcement received?*

❏ *How do you think the women felt about the disciples' reception of their announcement?*

4. (24:12) *What was Peter's response to what he saw? (John 20:3-9 indicates another apostle—probably John—ran with Peter.)*

❏ *According to I Corinthians 15:12-26, what difference does it make to us today that Jesus really did rise from the dead?*

JESUS TALKS WITH TWO DISCIPLES
(Luke 24:13-35)

*O*n the same day as the resurrection, Jesus met two disciples on the road to Emmaus. After discussing the events and the prophecies concerning the Messiah, they had supper together, and the two finally recognized Jesus.

1. (24:13-18) *What was the reaction of the two when Jesus began talking with them?*

2. (24:19-21) *What does it appear that Cleopas and his companion thought about Jesus at this point?*

❏ *It must have been an incredible experience to have the Son of God explain the Scriptures concerning Himself (Luke 24:32). What are some of the reasons that these two followers of Jesus did not better understand who Jesus was and the prophecies about Him?*

3. (24:30-31) *When did they recognize who Jesus was and why at that particular time? (In at least three instances, "breaking of bread" seems to have had spiritual significance— Jesus' feeding the 4,000, feeding the 5,000, and the Last Supper.)*

4. (24:33-35; see also Matthew 28:8-9) *List the followers of Jesus who by this time had seen Him since His resurrection.*

❏ *How do you think the eleven remaining apostles (Judas had committed suicide) felt after Cleopas and his friend recounted their experience?*

JESUS MEETS WITH ELEVEN APOSTLES
(Luke 24:36-49)

*I*n the Upper Room Jesus taught the disciples about the Messiah and explained how they were to serve Him.

1. (24:36-41) *Why might the eleven disciples have been so reluctant to believe in spite of all the testimony?*

2. (24:39-43) *Jesus' resurrected body was an actual body, but it was not restricted by physical limitations. What did Jesus do to demonstrate that He was not just a spirit?*

3. (24:44-45) *Why had the disciples not understood and applied the Scripture concerning the Messiah?*

❐ *Perhaps the idea of Messiah's suffering (at His First Coming) and glorification (at His Second Coming) confused the apostles. What would Jesus think about your understanding of the Scriptures?*

4. (24:46-49) *What important instructions did Jesus give to His apostles? (See also Acts 1:8 and the fulfillment in Acts 2.)*

JESUS ASCENDS INTO HEAVEN
(Luke 24:50-53)

After walking with His disciples to Bethany, Jesus ascended to Heaven and left the disciples to praise and serve Him. They would obey His great commission to them and begin His church upon the earth.

1. (24:52-53) *What brought about the dramatic change in the disciples' attitude?*

2. (24:51-53) *Why weren't the disciples devastated by Jesus leaving them again?*

❐ *What does their reaction teach us about how we should feel knowing Jesus is in Heaven, interceding for us today?*

DIGGING DEEPER

1. *In what ways might we be like the two disciples on the road to Emmaus?*

2. *What can you do to improve your understanding and application of Bible prophecies yet to be fulfilled?*

3. *If we know that Jesus died, rose again, and ascended into Heaven, what responsibility do we have toward others?*

4. *Look back at the parables Jesus told in chapters 11, 12, 13, 14, or 15 and rewrite one of them in contemporary language, reflecting the same spiritual truth. Could you use this to tell others about Jesus?*

5. *Spend a few moments reflecting on Jesus, who has died, who is risen, who will come again. Jot down some thoughts on what you can do to know Jesus, the risen Lord, more completely.*

❖